The Oceans of Florida

VOLUME 3
OF THE FLORIDA WATER STORY

Peggy Sias Lantz and Wendy A. Hale

Illustrated by Jean Barnes

Pineapple Press, Inc.
Sarasota, Florida

To my mother, who first taught me to love the written word. —Peggy Lantz

To Nikki and Chris, and our family's love of the sea. —Wendy Hale

To Mikey and in memory of Ruth E. and Albert G. Wilson —Jean Barnes

TABLE OF CONTENTS

Inquiries should be addressed to:
Pineapple Press, Inc.
P.O. Box 3889
Sarasota, Florida 34230

www.pineapplepress.com

First Edition
10 9 8 7 6 5 4 3 2 1

Design by Carol Tornatore
Illustrations colorized by Jennifer Borresen
Printed in the United States

Library of Congress Cataloging-in-Publication Data
Lantz, Peggy Sias, author.
    The oceans of Florida / Peggy Sias Lantz and Wendy Hale. — First edition.
        pages cm. — (The Florida water story series ; volume 3)
    Summary: "The abundance of marine life found in Florida's offshore waters is truly astonishing. More than 1,000 species of saltwater fish have been identified. Add to that number the invertebrates, algae, grasses, seaweeds, plankton, and all of the other creatures that call the ocean home, and you'll discover an amazing world of life surrounding you in Florida's oceans."—Provided by publisher.
    Audience: Ages 10–14.
    Audience: Grades 7 to 8.
    ISBN 978-1-56164-704-0 (pbk. : alk. paper)
    1. Marine animals—Atlantic Ocean—Juvenile literature. 2. Marine animals—Mexico, Gulf of—Juvenile literature. 3. Marine ecology—Atlantic Ocean—Juvenile literature. 4. Marine ecology—Mexico, Gulf of—Juvenile literature. 5. Natural history—Florida—Juvenile literature. 6. Florida Keys National Marine Sanctuary (Fla.)—Juvenile literature. 7. Dry Tortugas (Fla.)—Juvenile literature. I. Hale, Wendy, 1954– author. II. Title.

QH92.L36 2014
578.770973—dc23
                                            2014010161

Oceans

When we stand on the top of a sand dune and look out across the ocean to the distant horizon, most of us see just the vast shining ripples and rolling waves breaking and foaming as they approach the shore. Unless a fin breaks the surface or a seabird dives in to catch a meal, we can only wonder about what's underneath.

It's not until we take a plunge beneath the waves, perhaps wearing a snorkel and mask or scuba tank, that we find the ocean is alive with a fantastic variety of creatures. In fact, every part of the ocean supports some kind of plant or animal life—no matter how warm or cold, or how deep and dark, the water might be.

The abundance of marine life found in Florida's offshore waters is truly astonishing. Imagine— over 1,000 species of saltwater fish have been identified here! And that number doesn't include the invertebrates, the animals without backbones, such as snails and jellyfish; nor the algae, grasses, and seaweeds; nor the masses of single-celled plants and animals called plankton; nor all the other creatures that call the ocean home.

This book will introduce you to some of the plants and animals that live in the water surrounding Florida's shores. So, come on! Take the plunge, and see the "Oceans Alive" for yourself!

Where Is Offshore?

Offshore means the open water—away from the sand, mud, or rocks of the beach, past the shallow seagrass beds and mangrove forests, beyond the barrier islands and coral reefs—far out to sea. Sometimes referred to as pelagic, this vast open area of the ocean is by far the largest of all the world's ecosystems.

Fewer plants and animals live in offshore waters than closer to the coast. Plants and animals need nutrients to live and grow. Nutrients include nitrates, phosphates, and other chemicals, and come from silt and organic materials in the soil.

Close to land, Florida rivers and lagoons pour nutrients into the ocean through inlets, where billions of gallons of fresh and brackish water move in and out with the tides. Pelagic waters receive few of these nutrients, for by the time they reach far offshore, they are diluted by the vast quantities of salty water in the open ocean.

brackish   slightly salty.
inlet   a narrow waterway opening of the coastline.
nutrients   foods that promote growth.
organic   made of living (or formerly living) plants or animals.

ecosystem   communities of plants and animals that naturally grow and live together.
pelagic   referring to the open sea.
silt   a fine layer of mud and clay.

Ocean Motion

Ocean waters are constantly in motion. Waves at the surface are caused by many forces—including the up and down movement of tides, the fall of rain, and even earthquakes—but primarily by the wind.

Currents below the surface are caused by wind, gravity, and differences in salinity and temperature. Some ocean currents transport warm or cold water over thousands of miles, affecting the climate of the land they pass by. Currents also transport fish, sea turtles, seaweeds, and ships.

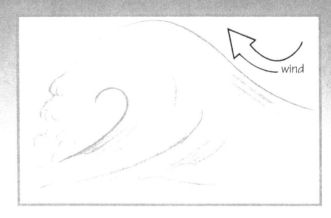

River in the Sea

One of the strongest warm-water currents in the world flows around Florida. Near the Florida coast the Gulf Stream is known as the Florida Current. Like a huge river in the sea, this strong current carries warm water from the Gulf of Mexico around the tip of Florida. It hugs the ocean side of the Florida Keys, then travels northward into the Atlantic Ocean, staying close to the coast—sometimes just a few miles offshore—until it reaches offshore of Cape Canaveral. This jutting land mass directs the current farther eastward and into the open ocean.

evaporation   changing from a liquid to a vapor.
salinity   the amount of salt in the water.

3

Florida's Atlantic Side

The broad, sandy beaches along Florida's Atlantic coast gradually slope to the sea. As the land disappears under the water, it becomes the continental shelf. It declines until it reaches a rim where the shelf begins to slope steeply to the ocean floor.

Hardbottom

The sand or mud-covered ocean floor has rocky areas, called hardbottom. This provides a firm surface that animals, such as corals and sponges, attach to.

Many sedentary animals that can't move on their own live here. They depend upon the currents to bring them food and to remove their wastes. Animals that can move roam over the hardbottom and use the cracks and holes as hiding places.

Sea turtles come to feed on the sponges, lobsters, and conchs that live on the hardbottom, and they rest underneath the clifflike overhangs. Some fish are permanent residents, while others use these areas only seasonally. Hardbottom areas close to the edge of the Florida Current are often good places for fishermen to catch snapper, grouper, and sea bass.

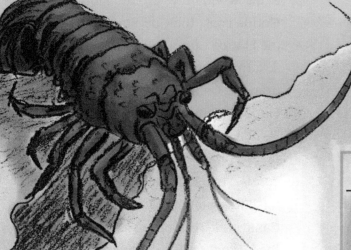

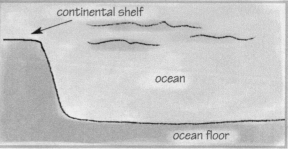

continental shelf

ocean

ocean floor

continental shelf   the sea bed surrounding a continent, the edge of which drops steeply to the ocean floor.

hardbottom   rocky areas of the sea floor.
sedentary   moving about very little.

A sponge is an animal

Sponges are simple animals that live on the hardbottom. Many sponges have glasslike skeletons that support a tough outer skin, giving them different shapes.

A sponge is a sessile animal, meaning it needs something—a shell, rock, or coral reef—to attach to. Instead of chasing food, it filters microscopic plants and animals through water canals in its body. It is porous—like a sponge!—with small pores, or holes, that let water and oxygen flow in. Larger pores allow wastes mixed in the seawater to flow out.

The sponge you use in your bath is probably synthetic, though people used to use real sponges. You can still buy bath sponges made from once-living animals, but they are quite expensive. If you should ever find a sponge on the beach or buy a real one in a store, remember this is the soft skeleton of an animal that once was firmly anchored to the sea floor.

Tube sponge

One of the sponges you can sometimes find while beach-combing is a tube sponge. It grows in a cluster of open-ended tubes and can be as long as your arm. It is pale blue when alive, but bleaches to a grayish white color when dead.

Red beard sponge

This colorful, orange-red sponge grows in beardlike strands on piers and pilings as well as on oyster-shell beds, shipwrecks, or hard-bottom in deeper water. Although this sponge is not harmful to people, other red or orange species sting, so avoid touching any brightly colored sponges.

microscopic   too small to be seen without a magnifying lens.
porous   having pores, or holes, through which water can flow.
sessile   referring to animals that require something to attach to.
species   a kind of plant or animal.
synthetic   not natural, but man-made by chemical processes.

Florida's Gulf Side

Sometimes called "America's Sea," the Gulf of Mexico covers some 1,500,000 kilometers (600,000 square miles), is over 3.2 kilometers (2 miles) deep, and borders Florida, four other states, and the country of Mexico. Along the west coast of Florida, the continental shelf extends in a broad, shallow expanse far out into the Gulf of Mexico.

Gulfside waters are often cloudy with silt and other particles, particularly near the mouths of large rivers where the incoming tide and outflowing river waters mix. Much of the Gulf bottom is mud and sand with few hardbottom communities, although storms and hurricanes sometimes expose more hard surfaces that animals and plants can colonize.

Living Seashells

Hard-shelled clam ⟶

Many species of clams inhabit offshore waters in the Gulf of Mexico. A clam uses a strong muscle, called a foot, to burrow deeply into the bottom. Clams are called bivalves because the soft parts of the clam are held inside two (bi-) hinged, hard shells, or valves.

Hard-shelled clams survive under difficult conditions. A clam larva must swim or crawl over the mud-covered bottom until it finds a suitable surface to attach to or burrow into.

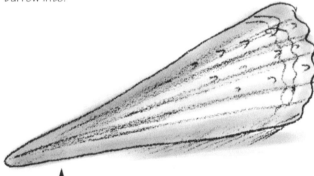

Pen shell

The pen shell lives with its narrow end buried in soft, sandy mud. It spins a thread that helps it attach to loose stones or broken shells along the bottom. If it is uprooted by a predator or a storm, its thin, brittle shell soon breaks, and you may find the pieces washed up on a nearby beach.

Perverse whelk

The perverse whelk is a snail that feeds on hard-shelled clams along the muddy bottoms of Florida's Gulf coast.

An adult whelk has a very heavy shell, often with spines near the top. If you hold most whelk species from the top, the hole is on the right. But the opening on the perverse whelk is on the left.

A female whelk lays a long string of egg capsules that look like little plastic pouches lined up in a row. One end of the string is cemented to a rock or dead shell, while the other end floats in the currents until the eggs hatch. As many as 100 tiny snails grow inside each pouch and soon escape into the sea through a hole near the top.

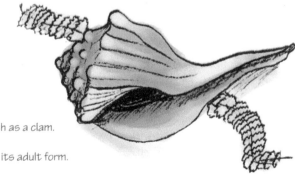

bivalve   an animal with two matching shells hinged together, such as a clam.
colonize   to settle as a group and grow in a new environment.
larva   an immature form of an animal that is very different from its adult form.
predator   an animal that hunts, kills, and eats other animals.

Dry Tortugas

Far out into the Gulf waters, more than 100 kilometers (70 miles) beyond the United States' southernmost city of Key West, lie seven small islands known as the Dry Tortugas. They were first named *Las Tortugas*—Spanish words meaning "the turtles"—because of the great numbers of sea turtles that used to be seen here. "Dry" was added later by sailors because no fresh water can be found on any of the islands.

The Dry Tortugas is now a national park and an important refuge for wildlife. It offers protection to a large colony of sooty terns, a species of seabird that nests here.

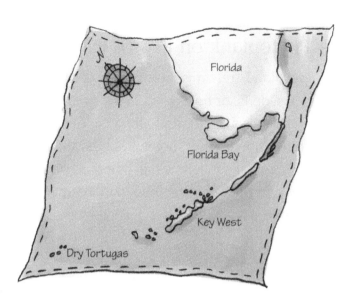

Sooties

Sooty terns are true pelagic birds that spend much of the year at sea. But during the nesting season they must find land. On Bush Key in the Dry Tortugas, more than 100,000 sooty terns nest closely together in a colony.

Called "wide-awakes" because of their nonstop calls, sooties busily raise their families from March, when eggs are laid, till September. Then the birds leave the island and fly thousands of miles across the open ocean to their winter home off the coast of Africa.

colony   *a group of the same kind of animal living together.*

7

Drifters

Phytoplankton (say "FIE-toe-plank-tun")

Most land creatures have homes of some sort—nests, dens, or holes—but in the ocean, billions of animals swim or drift along their entire lives, going with the flow. Some live near the surface, close to the sunlight, while others move up and down through the water column in order to capture whatever food is available.

Food for many ocean creatures—from tiny shrimp to the biggest whale—includes a living soup made of tiny microscopic plants and animals called plankton. Plant plankton is called phytoplankton, and animal plankton is called zooplankton.

Diatoms

One of the most important food sources in the ocean is a yellow-green alga. Billions of phytoplankton called diatoms drift in offshore waters. They enclose themselves in glassy, shell-like structures with beautiful shapes and patterns.

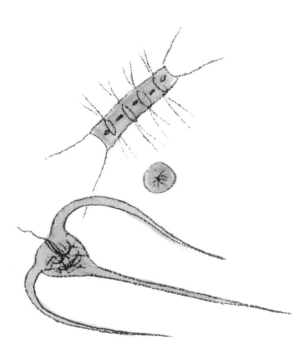

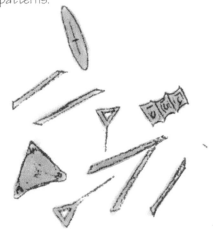

Dinoflagellates

Another important phytoplankton, called a dinoflagellate, looks like both a plant and an animal plankton. It swims instead of just drifting by propelling itself with a hairlike structure called a flagellum in grooves along its body. Diatoms and dinoflagellates are eaten by zooplankton and many larger creatures, such as oysters and clams.

alga   one of certain plants that usually live in water. The plural—algae—is used more often.
flagellum   a long, hairlike growth from a cell that helps it move.
phytoplankton   plant plankton.
plankton   microscopic plants and animals that drift in the sea.
water column   the space from the water surface to the ocean floor.
zooplankton   animal plankton.

Phytoplankton, a living soup

Phytoplankton is made up of tiny, usually single-celled plants. Phytoplankton uses the energy of the sun to make food, as all plants do.

The great mass of phytoplankton that drifts near the surface, closest to the sunlight, is the lowest line of the food chain. Animals that eat plants feed upon phytoplankton, and some of them are then eaten by other animals.

Plankton gone wild

Phytoplankton needs sunlight to grow, and it also needs certain essential nutrients in the water. But too many nutrients can create problems. During Florida's rainy season, fertilizers from farms and lawns and seepage from septic tanks run off the land into nearby waters, eventually reaching the deeper waters of the Gulf and the ocean. This can cause unusual growths of phytoplankton, called blooms, that prevent other marine plants and animals from receiving the sunlight and oxygen they need.

Red tide

Certain types of dinoflagellates cause occasional massive blooms, called red tide, that turns sea water a reddish brown color. Poisons produced by the dinoflagellates can kill fish and shellfish. Red tide can even cause the death of manatees and create breathing problems for people.

blooms unusually high growths of phytoplankton.
food chain the passage of food energy from plants, which make their own food from the energy of the sun, to animals that eat plants, to animals that eat other animals.

9

More Drifters

Zooplankton (say "ZOE-uh-plank-tun")

Zooplankton are animal plankton. During the day, zooplankton and other marine organisms move up the water column to feed upon phytoplankton found closer to the sunlight.

Some species of zooplankton are destined to stay plankton for their entire lives. They drift about in the open ocean feeding on other plankton and being eaten by fish, whales, crabs, and snails.

But other zooplankton are larvae and spend only part of their lives in this floating state. As they grow, they change. Leaving behind the characteristics of zooplankton, they eventually become adult worms, jellyfish, crabs, or barnacles, depending on their species.

Goose barnacles

A barnacle is a shrimplike animal encased within a shell made of hard, calcareous plates. A young barnacle begins life as a zooplankton, but soon settles onto a hard surface, such as a piling, a log, a drifting bottle, or even a sea turtle's back! Here it changes into a stalked, sessile animal protected by its hardened plates.

You can sometimes find goose barnacles attached to old boards, bottles, or other debris that washes up on the beach. Their name comes from an old myth that goose barnacles turned into geese, perhaps because the long stalk of the barnacle resembles a goose's neck.

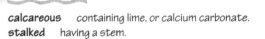

calcareous   containing lime, or calcium carbonate.
stalked   having a stem.

Glowing Waters

Sometimes at night ocean waters glow with a brilliant blue light that blinks on and off like a firefly. You can see it in a boat's wake on a dark night or when a big fish moves through the water. This glow, called bioluminescence, is produced by billions of plankton creatures.

Few bioluminescent creatures glow all night long, except when they want to attract prey or communicate. Most are invisible in the darkness until disturbed, when they turn on their special glow and light up the ocean.

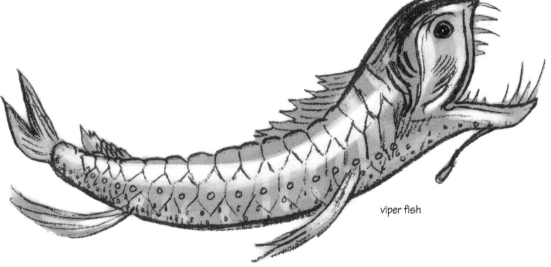

viper fish

angler fish

Fish that flash

Scientists believe that many deep-sea creatures are bioluminescent. The viper fish uses lights inside its mouth to lure prey into a trap. The angler fish wiggles a special lighted appendage—like a fishing pole—over its head to attract small fish who come to investigate and then become dinner. Other fish use their light to attract mates or to communicate with other members of their species.

appendage   an attached body part.
bioluminescence   light given off by living organisms.

Plants That Drift

Most marine plants are algae and are too small to be seen except under a microscope. But even those that are not microscopic are often difficult to identify because very few species of marine plants have flowers, roots, stems, or leaves as plants do on dry land.

Although few in number, marine plants are an important source of food and shelter to many other organisms.

Sargassum and fellow travelers

The golden-brown sargassum weed, or gulf weed, is a marine algae with berrylike floats that help it drift at sea. Huge masses of sargassum weed collect far off the Florida coast in a part of the Atlantic Ocean known as the Sargasso Sea. Sometimes you can find it washed ashore in large mats.

Some animals hitch a ride or find a home in floating seaweed drifting in the currents. Some camouflage themselves from attackers by taking on the color of the host plant. When storm winds or currents break loose clumps of sargassum, these clumps and their fellow travelers float along, making up a unique micro-community where several plants and animals live together in their own small world.

Sargassum crabs

These crabs live in mid-ocean, hitching a ride with sargassum weed in the Gulf Stream currents. In fact, the scientific name of one species means "little wanderer." Waving its tiny claws about the berrylike floats, it eats some of its fellow travelers.

12   **micro-community**   a small, specialized habitat of plants and animals.

Sea slugs

Nudibranchs, sometimes called sea slugs, are among the most beautiful marine creatures, in spite of their not-so-beautiful name. They are related to the more familiar snail or clam, though most nudibranchs do not have an external shell.

The sargassum nudibranch lives in sargassum weed. Its olive-brown body with specks of white, orange, and brown allows it to blend in with the golden stalks of its plant host.

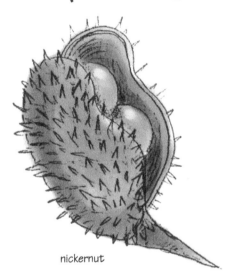

nickernut

Sea beans

Seeds from marine and land plants drift in the ocean. Sea beans are the seeds of tropical vines and trees that fell from the parent plant on an island or in a rainforest and washed out to sea. They may drift with the Gulf Stream and other ocean currents for a long time before finally washing onto a beach thousands of miles away.

The sea bean most commonly found on Florida beaches is sometimes called the hamburger bean, because it has a dark stripe around the middle that appears to be held between two lighter-colored "buns."

hamburger bean

sea heart

Seaweed suppers

Marine plants are important to people, too. Many cultures use certain seaweeds every day in the foods they prepare. You might not know that you eat seaweed in ice cream and chocolate milk, and use it in toothpaste, cosmetics, and certain medicines. Other seaweeds are ground up and used for animal feed, fertilizers, and garden mulch.

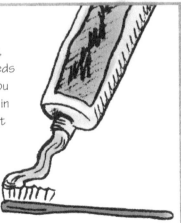

 nudibranch   a sea slug whose name means "bare gills."

Animals That Drift

Even though water is their home, many animals that live in the ocean are not good swimmers. Like plankton and marine plants, many invertebrates depend on the waves and currents to move them about, although some can also move under their own power.

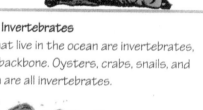

Invertebrates

Many of the animals that live in the ocean are invertebrates, meaning they have no backbone. Oysters, crabs, snails, and jellyfish are all invertebrates.

Blue buttons

Tiny, round, pale-blue discs called blue buttons float on the surface of tropical waters and sometimes wash up on Florida beaches by the thousands. About the size of a quarter, these harmless little jellyfish are fringed with delicate blue tentacles.

By-the-wind-sailor

Also called Velella, this tiny, violet-colored jellyfish has air chambers that allow it to float and a transparent triangular fin that extends above the suface, like a sail, to catch the wind and blow it along.

There's no shortage of these jellyfish in the sea. A ship reported sailing through and being surrounded by Velella for five solid days, as it travelled nearly 3700 kilometers (2,000 nautical miles)!

Swimming sea snails and sea slugs eat by-the-wind-sailors and blue buttons. By attacking and feeding on the tiny tentacles from underneath, they are unharmed by the stinging cells.

invertebrate   any animal without a backbone.
marine   in or about the sea.
nautical mile   a measurement used in ocean navigation, equal to 1852 meters (6076 feet).
tentacles   a ring of food-gathering appendages surrounding the mouth of some marine animals.

Neither jelly nor fish

A jellyfish floats gracefully through the sea with long tentacles trailing beneath it, or swims by opening and closing its body wall like an umbrella.

Jellyfish are not fish at all. They vary in size, shape, and color, but many look like plastic bags filled with a squishy, jellylike material.

Most jellyfish have stinging cells, called nematocysts, on tentacles that rim the mouth. Each nematocyst is like a miniature harpoon loaded with poison that can be shot out to catch plankton, small fish, or even other jellyfish. Each nematocyst is used only once, and a new stinging cell grows to take its place.

Cannonball jellyfish

Growing nearly to the size of a bowling ball (or cannonball, in the days when it was named) this brownish jellyfish is a strong swimmer. Under water, its jellylike material appears very thick and looks like half an egg—a very big egg!

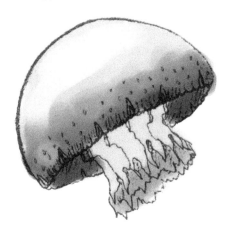

Comb jelly cowboys

A comb jelly gets its name from the rows of fringed hairs, resembling tiny combs, that beat together to propel it through the water. Although it has no stinging nematocysts, a comb jelly can rope and kill other sea jellies and small fish using special sticky cells, called lasso cells, that latch onto the prey as it swims by.

Small, delicate, and beautiful to look at, a comb jelly catches the sunlight and refracts it, creating rainbow colors along its translucent body. Comb jellies are also bioluminescent and flash in the water at night.

Deadly balloons

Beachcombers in Florida often find the beautiful but dangerous Portuguese man-of-war jellyfish washed up on the beach, looking like a harmless purple balloon. If you step on one of them, the float makes a popping sound, but you will regret it. Touching the tentacles causes severe pain. Swimmers in the ocean should be on the lookout for the animal's long tentacles, armed with powerful stinging cells. Tentacles may trail out behind as much as 15 meters (50 feet)! Alive or dead, Portuguese-men-of-war always should be avoided.

nematocysts   stinging cells in the tentacles of coral polyps, jellyfish, and anemones.
refract   to change the direction of a light wave.
translucent   allowing light to partially pass through.

15

What eats a jellyfish?

Although it may seem hard to believe, the world's largest sea turtle lives on a diet of jellyfish! The leatherback sea turtle can dive to great depths—more than 300 meters (1,000 feet)—in search of jellyfish. Stiff spines in its throat project backwards to help the turtle swallow its soft prey.

Sea turtles sometimes mistake plastic in the ocean—sandwich bags or balloons floating on the surface—for soft-bodied animals such as the Portuguese-man-of-war. If a leatherback eats the plastic, it could die.

prey   an animal that is eaten by another animal.

Swimmers

Some zooplankton, when they grow into adults, join the ranks of free-swimming creatures of the sea. Plankton move at the mercy of the currents, but the swimmers of the ocean are streamlined and move independently of ocean currents.

Fish facts

Most fish begin their lives as tiny eggs adrift in the sea. Larvae develop inside the eggs, and when they hatch they feed on plankton until they develop into young fish.

Fish are cold-blooded animals that breathe through gills and have fins instead of arms and legs. They are vertebrates, and most fish have skeletons made of bone. A few, such as sharks, rays, and skates, have cartilage instead of bone. We have cartilage in our bodies, too—push gently on your ear or the end of your nose to feel it!

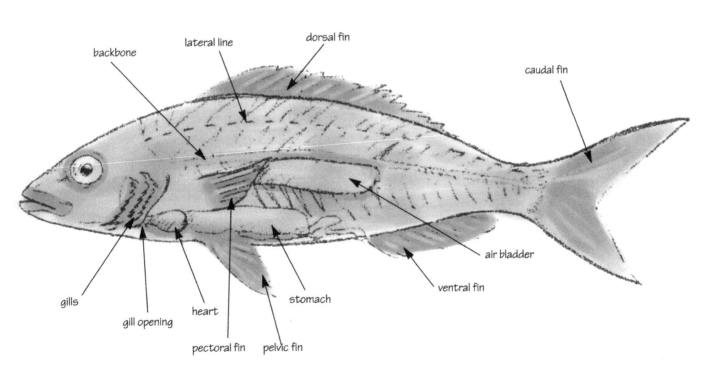

backbone · lateral line · dorsal fin · caudal fin · gills · gill opening · heart · pectoral fin · pelvic fin · stomach · ventral fin · air bladder

cartilage   semi-hard, elastic-like tissue that takes the place of a skeleton in some animals.
vertebrate   an animal with a backbone.

Fish Features

Survival is the name of the game for all animals, including those that live in the sea. Many fish have unique—even bizarre—ways to survive.

Barbels

Barbels may look like whiskers, but they are feelers that help a fish find and taste food. The black drum has 10 to 14 pairs of tiny barbels on its chin. The sea catfish has 4-6 long barbels around its mouth.

Ocean colors

Some skates and rays show patterns of color that help them avoid animals that might eat them. Seen from above, dark backs blend in with the dark color of the deep ocean. From below, predators have difficulty seeing light bellies against the brighter, sunlit surface.

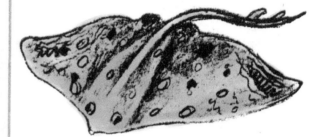

Spines

Some slow-swimming fish, such as the scorpionfish, have sharp or poisonous spines along their backs for protection. A stingray has a poisonous spine on its tail.

The ocean triggerfish gets its name from the first of three stiff spines along its dorsal fin. When it is disturbed, this spine locks upright like a trigger.

Shock treatment

Several fish have special body organs that produce electricity used in defense. The star-gazer has electrical cells in the top of its head. It lies buried in the sand where its electric organ helps it to sense and, if necessary, shock nearby predators.

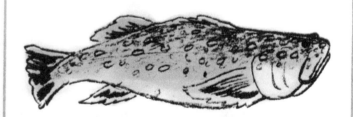

The balloon trick

The puffer fish can inflate its body like a balloon, making it appear larger than it really is. When threatened, the puffer can "blow up" to three times its normal size, too big for many predators to swallow. When the danger is gone, it deflates and swims away.

barbels   the slender bristles on the mouths of certain fish.

18   dorsal fin   the main fin on the top, or back, of a fish.

Florida Fishes

Flying fish

A fish that can fly? Well, not really, but a flying fish can look like it's flying. It vibrates its long tail in the water until its extended, winglike fins are above the surface, giving the fish enough lift to skim above the water.

It may leave the water at 48 to 64 kilometers (30 to 40 miles) per hour, gliding for 30 seconds and traveling 90 meters (300 feet) before it dives back into the ocean. Flying fish do this mainly to escape from larger fish, such as tuna or dolphin, that eat them.

Don't confuse me with Flipper!

The dolphin, or dorado, is a blue, yellow, and gold fish that should never be confused with the marine mammal that has the same name. The dolphin fish has a blunt forehead and is one of the fastest fishes in the sea, with speeds estimated at more than 80 kilometers (50 miles) per hour!

Bluefish

Bluefish, named for their silvery-blue color, travel in large schools and feed on smaller fish. They have sharp teeth, and if you happen to be in the surf when "the blues are running," you could accidentally be grazed or cut during their feeding frenzy!

Snappers

Snappers are important to Florida fishermen. Although they live mainly in tropical waters, some species are wide ranging. They can grow into very large fish, and often spend their time patrolling the hardbottom, reefs, and wrecks where smaller fish like to hide.

The mutton snapper has a small spot on the side of its pinkish body. It is a prized seafood and is often sold in markets as red snapper.

Life on the Ocean Floor

Some animals, instead of drifting along in the currents or propelling themselves under their own power, live on the ocean floor. These bottom dwellers that slink, slither, and crawl are called benthic animals.

Benthic animals never venture far up the water column. Most of them are dull in color, and some spend their entire lives on, or just beneath, the sea floor. Here, where water movement is weak and no pounding waves or tossing currents can harm their bodies, animals are often quite delicate.

When a swimming animal or a floating seaweed dies, it joins a slow rain of other dead animals, plants, and wastes that drift down to the bottom of the sea. For many benthic animals, this detritus is their main source of food.

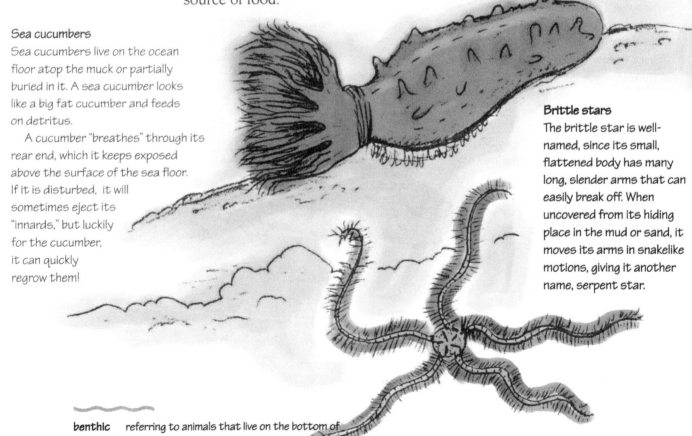

Sea cucumbers

Sea cucumbers live on the ocean floor atop the muck or partially buried in it. A sea cucumber looks like a big fat cucumber and feeds on detritus.

A cucumber "breathes" through its rear end, which it keeps exposed above the surface of the sea floor. If it is disturbed, it will sometimes eject its "innards," but luckily for the cucumber, it can quickly regrow them!

Brittle stars

The brittle star is well-named, since its small, flattened body has many long, slender arms that can easily break off. When uncovered from its hiding place in the mud or sand, it moves its arms in snakelike motions, giving it another name, serpent star.

benthic referring to animals that live on the bottom of the ocean.

detritus particles of decayed animals and plants.

Animal "flowers"

Anemones belong to the jellyfish and coral group. In its early life, an anemone is a free-swimming planktonic animal. But it spends the adult part of its life as a large polyp, attached to a hardbottom with its tentacles waving to catch prey. If touched, most anemones shrink down into a soft blob.

Just like certain sea jellies, anemones use nematocysts, or stinging cells, to capture plankton or small fish. Some fish, however, can safely live among the stinging tentacles and not be harmed by them. The anemone provides protection and food scraps for the fish, and in turn, the fish lures other creatures into the anemone's tentacles. Both the fish and the anemone benefit from this relationship.

How do we know who lives on the bottom?

An average diver with a scuba tank can dive to only about 60 meters (200 feet). The pressure of the sea water is usually too great for most people to tolerate. How, then, can we know what life is like far below on the sea floor?

Scientists have designed machines called remotely operated vehicles, or ROVs, that are lowered from research ships to the sea floor. Like tethered robots, their specially-mounted television cameras show us the fascinating world of the deep ocean.

polyp   a marine animal with a tubelike body which is attached at one end to a hard surface and which has a mouth at the other end.

21

Dangers in the Deep

Many sea creatures eat other living animals to survive. An animal that kills other animals for food is called a predator.

Sharks

Sharks are the most well known and feared of the predators. With more than 250 species, the shark family is huge and varied. It includes the plankton-eating whale shark weighing 11,000 kilograms (12 tons) and the tiny, 25-centimeter (10-inch) long, smooth dogfish.

Most sharks are torpedo-shaped and covered with tiny, teethlike scales that make them feel as rough as sandpaper. A shark's powerful tail speeds its streamlined shape through the water.

A shark is both a carnivore and a scavenger. It relies on vision, a keen sense of smell, and an ability to detect movement to find food in murky waters.

Most sharks find food scarce on the bottom. Though they will sometimes rest on the bottom, or swim just above it looking for benthic animals to eat, they may have to eat one another instead, or move hundreds of feet up the water column to find smaller fish to prey upon.

Tiger shark

With stripes like a tiger, this large predator often grows to 4 meters (14 feet) or more. It feeds on all kinds of sea life, including rays and even other sharks.

Unlike certain shark species that lay eggs in leathery cases, the tiger shark gives birth to live young, but the mother does not care for them once they are born.

Smooth dogfish

The smooth dogfish swims in huge schools in shallow waters, searching for sick or injured fish, lobsters, and crabs. Its small teeth grind together to crush the hard shells.

Shark's teeth

A shark constantly sheds worn-out teeth and grows new ones. With three to fifteen sets of teeth neatly arranged in its jaw, a shark may go through as many as 30,000 teeth in a lifetime!

You can find ancient shark's teeth on some Florida beaches. Sizes range from the tiny teeth of the sharp-nosed shark to the hand-sized teeth of the extinct giant white shark.

carnivore an animal that eats other animals.
scavenger an animal that feeds on dead animals.

Look out!

Swimmers and fishermen watch for fins breaking the surface of the water. Each shark species has its own shape of fin, but not all of the fins you see sticking out of the water belong to sharks. Porpoises, dolphins, skates, and rays sometimes show their fins above water.

Shark suckers

The remora, or shark sucker, is a fish that attaches itself to sharks or other large fish for a free ride and for any leftover dinner scraps.

Its unusual, oval-shaped suction disc flaps open to create the suction the remora needs to attach to its host.

Skating along

Skates, stingrays, and manta rays all have flat bodies with skeletons made of cartilage (like sharks) and winglike pectoral fins that help them swim gracefully through the water. Most live near the sea bottom, where they feed on shellfish, worms, and crabs.

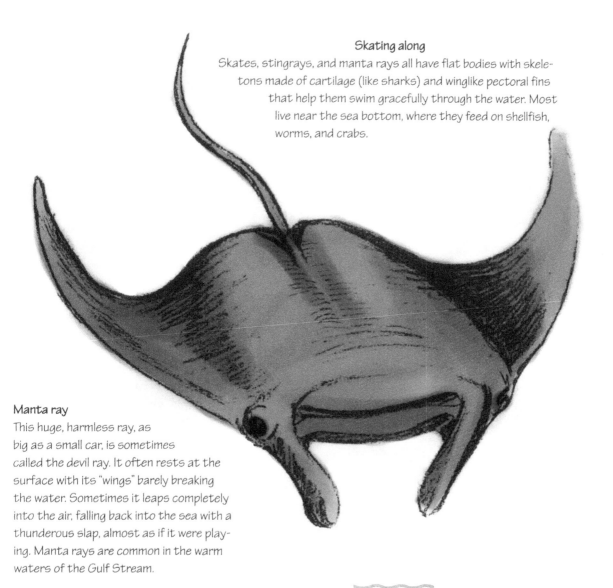

Manta ray

This huge, harmless ray, as big as a small car, is sometimes called the devil ray. It often rests at the surface with its "wings" barely breaking the water. Sometimes it leaps completely into the air, falling back into the sea with a thunderous slap, almost as if it were playing. Manta rays are common in the warm waters of the Gulf Stream.

pectoral fins   a pair of lower fins toward the front of a fish's body.

Marine Mammals

Of all the creatures that live in Florida's offshore waters, the marine mammals—whales, dolphins, and manatees—seem to fascinate us most.

They are warm-blooded animals of the sea that breathe air, have hair, and feed and care for their young. Special adaptations enable them to live in their watery world. Layers of blubber help them cope with cold ocean temperatures, for even around Florida the water is cold in the winter.

Whales and dolphins dive to great depths to capture food. Their bodies are built to survive the pressures of deep water. To communicate with one another, they make unusual sounds by forcing air through closed nasal cavities. They also reflect sounds off the ocean floor, like echoes, to help them find their way through murky ocean waters.

Southern right whale

One of the largest animals in the ocean gets all the nourishment it needs from feeding on the tiniest animals. The gigantic southern right whale strains microscopic zooplankton through huge baleen plates in its mouth. The whale forces water out through the plates to trap food. Then the whale licks the plankton off the baleen with its tongue and swallows it.

The southern right whale is an endangered species that migrates by Florida's Atlantic coast during the winter. A narrow strip of ocean water between Cape Canaveral and the Georgia-Florida border is its only known calving ground.

Long ago when whaling ships sailed the seas, sailors named these animals right whales because they were the "right" whales to kill. They swam slowly, which made them easier to catch, and when they died they floated, which made it easier to tow their carcasses. Even though by international agreement the right whale is no longer hunted by most nations, it still faces the danger of being struck by a ship as it swims along the surface.

baleen plates   horny material that hangs in fringed plates from the upper jaw of certain whales (also called whalebone).
blubber   fatty tissue in whales and their relatives.
calving ground   a place where female marine mammals give birth to their calves. (It's in the water even though it's called "ground.")

mammal   an animal that has a backbone and hair, and that gives birth and cares for its young.
nasal cavities   air passages in the nose.

Bottlenosed dolphin

Some marine mammals use sharp teeth to capture and eat squid and fish. Dolphins and porpoises belong to this group, and many people use these names interchangeably. But most commonly, those species with long beaklike jaws and cone-shaped teeth are called dolphins, while those without a beak and with broad, flat teeth are called porpoises.

There are many species of dolphin, but the bottlenosed dolphin is probably most familiar to us. We see it "surfing" in the bow waves of ships and performing at marine aquariums. Like most marine mammals, it is very intelligent and can memorize tricks and solve simple problems, such as maneuvering though an underwater maze.

The dolphin has a triangular-shaped dorsal fin that looks very much like a shark fin when you see it cutting through the water. But dolphins are a shark's natural enemy in the ocean. When gangs of dolphins ram a shark, one after another, they can chase it away and sometimes even kill it.

bow wave   waves made by the front of a boat.

Ocean Flyers

Seabirds live on or near the sea and get their food from it, either close to the coast or far offshore. They include familiar pelicans, gulls, and terns, as well as lesser-known petrels and gannets.

Although seabirds roam the world's oceans, we have limited knowledge of these far-ranging birds because they usually fly far from the sight of land. Yet the numbers of ocean-going birds stun the imagination. In fact, one of the smallest seabirds, the Wilson's storm-petrel, may be the world's most abundant bird!

Most seabirds have long, narrow wings to help them soar and glide effortlessly over the wave-tossed ocean. Their webbed feet act as brakes and assist in take-offs from the water.

Even though they spend most of their time at sea, they must return to land to raise their families, often gathering in huge colonies. They usually nest on remote islands or rugged cliffs where predators are few.

Storm-petrels

The storm-petrel has long legs in proportion to its small size. It flutters about with its legs dangling and feet pitter-pattering over the waves, as if it were walking on the water.

The storm-petrel belongs to a family of birds known as "tube-noses," because its nostrils extend in tubes along the outside of its bill. Tube-nosed birds get rid of excess salt in their bodies through these nasal cavities, and also use them to sniff out dead floating fish—food—from a great distance.

Gannets

The gannet, a large white and black seabird, flies off Florida's coast during the winter. It can dive from a considerable height, sometimes 30 meters (100 feet) or more, plunging beneath the surface to catch a mackerel or a flying fish in its powerful bill.

The telltale flash of white feathers alerts other gannets to the fishing action, and in no time others join the feeding frenzy. After eating, gannets often rest together on the water in loose flocks called rafts.

Frigatebirds

Not all seabirds catch their own fish. The magnificent frigatebird, also called the man-o'-war bird because of its warlike thievery, is a pirate who steals its meal from other seabirds.

With a deeply forked tail and long narrow wings that spread to over seven feet, the frigatebird soars and chases other seabirds for their food. It can also snatch flying fish or other food from the surface, but cannot swim or dive. In fact, it quickly becomes waterlogged if it rests on the surface, so the frigatebird must return to land at night to roost.

During the breeding season the male frigatebird inflates a balloonlike red patch of skin on his throat, which certainly must impress any female frigatebird nearby!

raft   a group of seabirds resting on the water.
roost   to rest or sleep on a perch or branch.   27

Migration and the "Little Guys"

Besides seabirds, which spend their entire lives flying over the world's oceans, other birds cross this vast open space twice each year. Millions of warblers, thrushes, and other songbirds fly high above Florida's offshore waters on their journey between summer nesting grounds in North America and winter homes on Caribbean islands or in Central or South America.

The journey is a difficult one, with the dangers of high winds and storms and the threat of exhaustion from flying nonstop over hundreds of kilometers of open water. Many small songbirds needing a rest find an island, the deck of a ship, or an oil-drilling platform to land on along the way.

Hurricane!

More hurricanes strike Florida than any other state, so it's no wonder that the Florida peninsula has been called "Hurricane Alley."

Hurricanes always form over offshore waters, because they depend on warm ocean temperatures and certain weather conditions. Most of the hurricanes that strike Florida's coast develop far out in the Atlantic Ocean, although some begin in the Caribbean Sea or Gulf of Mexico. How do the animals and plants living offshore deal with these powerful ocean storms?

peninsula   a narrow strip of land jutting into the ocean from the mainland.

Birds in the wind

Most seabirds fly out of the path of a hurricane. However, the violent winds sometimes hurl birds great distances through the air or across the sea.

Some species, such as the smaller and lighter storm-petrels or terns, may be "wrecked" ashore and later discovered wandering about dazed in the streets of inland towns. After a Florida hurricane we often hear reports of birds that have been blown far from their usual territories.

Sea creatures

Fish, whales, and most benthic animals have few problems with violent storms. Those living closer to the surface, however, near the powerful winds and waves, have a greater risk of injury during a hurricane.

In shallow seas, hurricane-spawned waves and currents can scour the sea floor, breaking coral and covering hardbottom communities and seagrass beds with a choking cover of silt and sand. Seaweeds and other marine plants can be torn apart and moved great distances from their original location.

Sea beans, nuts, and seeds from other countries wash ashore on Florida beaches or are blown far inland on the winds of a hurricane, sometimes sprouting in their new location.

Marine Conservation

For the ocean and its wildlife, the damaging effects of natural events such as hurricanes or red tides seem short-lived. But as we learn more about the fascinating world of the sea, we realize that human actions, too, affect the health of the ocean and its plants and animals.

On Florida beaches we find litter either thrown from ships and boats miles offshore or carried by ocean currents from far away. Dolphins and seabirds are caught in abandoned nets, and tangled fishing line traps fish and other animals. Snapper, shrimp, and clams become more difficult to catch each year because of overfishing. Ships and oil-drilling operations spill chemicals into the ocean, polluting the water and poisoning animals.

If we care about the ocean environment, we must be willing to protect Florida's offshore waters through beach cleanups and litter patrols, responsible fishing, and letters to local newspapers and politicians about stopping pollution. What ideas do you have for safe-guarding the sea?

Working together, we can keep the oceans and the creatures that live there alive and healthy so kids in the future also can share in the wonders of the sea.

31

Glossary

alga (AL-guh)   one of certain plants that usually live in water. The plural — algae (AL-jee) — is used more often.

appendage   an attached body part.

baleen plates   horny material that hangs in fringed plates from the upper jaw of certain whales (also called whalebone).

barbels (BAR-buls)   the slender bristles on the mouths of certain fish.

benthic   referring to animals that live on the bottom of the ocean.

bioluminescence (bi-oh-loom-in-ESS-ins)   light given off by living organisms.

bivalve   an animal with two matching shells hinged together, such as a clam.

blooms   unusually high growths of phytoplankton.

blubber   fatty tissue in whales and their relatives.

bow wave   the waves made by the front of a boat.

brackish   slightly salty.

calcareous (kal-KARE-ee-us)   containing lime, or calcium carbonate.

calving ground   a place where female marine mammals give birth to their calves. (It's in the water even though it's called "ground.")

carnivore   an animal that eats other animals.

cartilage   semi-hard, elastic-like tissue that takes the place of a skeleton in some animals.

colonize   to settle as a group and grow in a new environment.

colony   a group of the same kind of animal living together.

continental shelf   the sea bed surrounding a continent, the edge of which drops steeply to the ocean floor.

detritus (de-TRY-tus)   particles of decayed animals and plants.

dorsal fin   the main fin on the top, or back, of a fish.

ecosystem   communities of plants and animals that naturally grow and live together.

evaporation   changing from a liquid to a vapor.

flagellum (fla-JEL-lum)   a long, hairlike growth from a cell that helps it move.

food chain   the passage of food energy from plants, which make their own food from the energy of the sun, to animals that eat plants, to animals that eat other animals.

hardbottom   rocky areas of the sea floor.

inlet   a narrow waterway opening of the coastline.

invertebrate   any animal without a backbone.

larva (plural: larvae [LARV-eye])   the immature form of an animal that is very different from its adult form.

mammal   an animal that has a backbone and hair, and that gives birth and cares for its young.

marine   in or about the sea.

micro-community   a small, specialized habitat of plants and animals.

microscopic   too small to be seen without a magnifying lens.

nasal cavities   air passages in the nose.

nautical mile   a measurement used in ocean navigation, equal to 1852 meters (6076 feet).

nematocysts (nee-MAT-uh-sists)   stinging cells in the tentacles of coral polyps, jellyfish, and anemones.

nudibranch (NOOD-uh-brank)   a sea slug whose name means "bare gills."

nutrients (NOO-tree-ints)   foods that promote growth.

organic   made of living (or formerly living) plants and animals.

pectoral fins   a pair of lower fins toward the front of a fish's body.

pelagic (puh-LAJ-ik)   referring to the open sea.

peninsula   a narrow strip of land jutting into the ocean from the mainland.

phytoplankton (FIE-toe-plank-ton)   plant plankton.

plankton   microscopic plants and animals that drift in the sea.

polyp (PAUL-lip)   a marine animal with a tubelike body which is attached at one end to a hard surface and which has a mouth at the other end.

porous   having pores, or holes, through which water can flow.

predator   an animal that hunts, kills, and eats other animals.

prey   an animal that is eaten by another animal.

raft   a group of seabirds resting on the water.

refract   to change the direction of a light wave.

roost   to rest or sleep on a perch or branch.

salinity   the amount of salt in the water.

scavenger   an animal that feeds on dead animals.

sedentary   moving about very little.

sessile (SESS-ul)   referring to animals that require something to attach to.

silt   a fine layer of mud and clay.

species (SPEE-sheez)   a kind of plant or animal.

stalked   having a stem.

synthetic   not natural, but man-made by chemical processes.

tentacles   a ring of food-gathering appendages surrounding the mouth of some marine animals.

translucent   allowing light to partially pass through.

vertebrate   an animal with a backbone.

water column   the space from the water surface to the ocean floor.

zooplankton (ZOE-uh-plank-ton)   animal plankton.

CPSIA information can be obtained at www.ICGtesting.com
Printed in the USA
BVOW10s1206150414

350699BV00001B/4/P